HENRY'S FORK

Henry's Fork

Larry Tullis

Frank Amato

PORTLAND

River Journal

Volume 3, Number 1, 1995

About The Author

Larry Tullis is a professional outdoor writer/photographer from Orem, Utah. His writing and photography is found in magazines like *Flyfishing, Fly Fisherman, Flyfisher, Outdoor Photographer, Angler's Sport Calendars, Trout* (Stackpole Books), *Utah Fishing, Sports Guide* etc. His books include a previous River Journal volume on the "Green River" and one of the Lefty's Little Library Of Fly Fishing books on "Small Fly Techniques." He is currently working on several other books about nymphing, fly tying and Alaska rainbows.

Larry most recently guided in Alaska and previously on the Green River in Utah, the Henry's Fork, Idaho and the Madison, Montana. Larry has fished the Henry's Fork since the 70s and got his first fly fishing guide job working for Will Godfrey's Fly Fishing Center, on the Henry's Fork. He has loved and fished this famous river before and since.

◆

Acknowledgments

To all those who I have fished with and learned from, I give a general thanks but there are several individuals who have especially helped me and opened up the river's secrets to me.

I met Will Godfrey through a mutual friend when we fished Pyramid Lake in Nevada. We talked fishing, and though I was young and somewhat inexperienced, he hired me to work his fly shop on the Henry's Fork and to guide his clients. He had been one of the first fly fishing guides in the area when working out of West Yellowstone. His was the first fly shop on the river and he was largely responsible for the special regulations that helped preserve this remarkable waterway. His training has stayed with me and benefited me throughout my career in the fly fishing industry. I'll always be grateful to him for giving me my start in such a good, professional and personable way.

Owner of Henry's Fork Angler's, Mike Lawson's name has become synonymous with the Henry's Fork, not only because of his successful fly shop and expert guide service, or his expertise with a fly rod or developing fly patterns but because he is one of those rare characters who becomes a part of the river because of his concern, conservation efforts and influence on those who frequent the fishery. He provided me with invaluable information on the evolution of the river and convinced me that the future of the Henry's Fork is bright indeed.

Thanks to Lynn Sessions of Last Chance Outfitters for his help in getting some of the photos for this book. We guided together on the Green River in Utah and Lynn is always a friend of the river.

I'd also like to thank Bill Christensen and the boys of the Flat Rock Club. Bill introduced me to this comfortable and exclusive lodge where the effects of the members have been felt for nearly 100 years. It was the first fly fishing club in the area and its members have always practiced and preached conservation, its members have contributed much to the Henry's Fork Foundation and other efforts to preserve and enhance the fishery.

So many other friends and acquaintances have contributed to my education and enjoyment of this river that they cannot all be named. Writers who frequented the Henry's Fork, such as the late Charlie Brooks, Rene Harrop, Doug Swisher, Carl Richards, Ernie Schwiebert and many others, have inspired and educated a generation of anglers that may have never met the writers themselves. A special thanks to them because, as the late great Lee Wulff said, "A river without friends is a river without protection."

Last but definitely not least, I'd like to thank Frank Amato for encouraging me with this and other writing projects. We fished the Henry's Fork together and have had some great discussions around the camp in other areas such as his favorite river, the Deschutes in Oregon.

◆

Series Editor: Frank Amato — Kim Koch

Subscriptions:
Softbound: $29.90 for one year (four issues), $55.00 for two years
Hardbound Limited Editions: $80.00 one year, $150.00 for two years
Frank Amato Publications, Inc. • P.O. Box 82112 • Portland, Oregon 97282 • (503) 653-8108

Design: Joyce Herbst
Photographs: Larry Tullis
Fly Plates: Jim Schollmeyer • Map: Tony Amato
Printed in Hong Kong
Softbound ISBN:1-878175-79-3, Hardbound ISBN:1-878175-80-7
(Hardbound Edition Limited to 500 Copies)

HENRY'S FORK

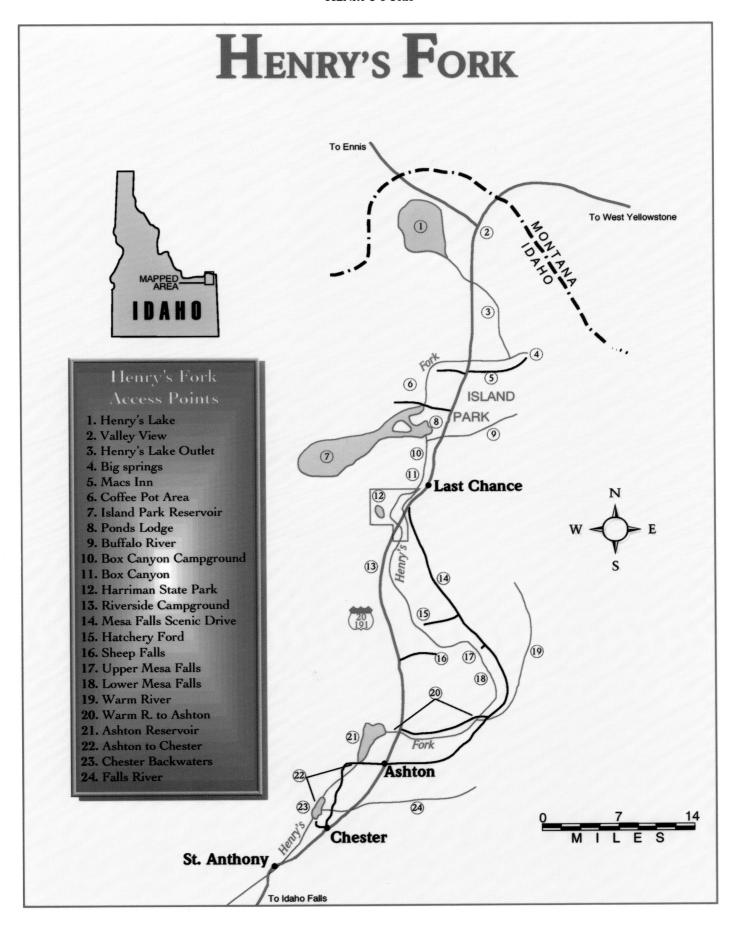

MAPPED
AREA
IDAHO

To Ennis

To West Yellowstone

MONTANA
IDAHO

ISLAND
PARK

Last Chance

N
W   E
S

**Henry's Fork
Access Points**

1. Henry's Lake
2. Valley View
3. Henry's Lake Outlet
4. Big springs
5. Macs Inn
6. Coffee Pot Area
7. Island Park Reservoir
8. Ponds Lodge
9. Buffalo River
10. Box Canyon Campground
11. Box Canyon
12. Harriman State Park
13. Riverside Campground
14. Mesa Falls Scenic Drive
15. Hatchery Ford
16. Sheep Falls
17. Upper Mesa Falls
18. Lower Mesa Falls
19. Warm River
20. Warm R. to Ashton
21. Ashton Reservoir
22. Ashton to Chester
23. Chester Backwaters
24. Falls River

20
191

Ashton

Fork

Chester

Henry's

St. Anthony

To Idaho Falls

0   7   14
MILES

Mike Lawson scanning the "Ranch" waters for regular risers.

HENRY'S FORK

◆

*T*HE GLASSY SURFACE GAVE LITTLE HINT OF THE intricate currents that interacted with fly, leader and line. Four fly patterns: an Adams, a No-Hackle Dun, a Green Drake Nymph, and a Spent-Wing Spinner had already been tried and the feeding pattern of the large bank feeding rainbow was unchanged. It fed with a rhythm known only to itself, ignoring good and bad fly presentations alike.

The weather was unsettled and a little breezy but now there was a stillness in the air. A thunderstorm was approaching and a light rain had dampened the meadow vegetation. Each breath now unconsciously registered the pungent scent of sage, pine and sweet grasses.

The trout's nose dimpled the surface again and again. Bending over to examine the water more closely, I used an aquarium net and quickly caught several species of mayflies represented by emergers, duns and spent-wing adults in the surface film. What was this trout feeding on? One of the mayfly emergers in the net broke free of its husk and began pumping fluid into its wings, always an amazing metamorphosis to watch. Some micro-caddis were also skimming the river's surface...maybe the trout was feeding on them. One more glance at the net found another insect hidden under a spent mayfly. It was a flying ant! Eureka!

I have seldom seen a trout that could resist an ant, when they were available. My terrestrial fly box revealed several flying ant patterns and one of approximately the right size and color was tied onto the 6X tippet. The down-and-across stream cast was almost right on. I raised the rod slightly and the fly drug into the feeding lane four feet above the delicate bulge that gave away the trout's location. Quickly dropping the rod, the fly drifted naturally to the fish. A subtle, almost invisible dimple made the fly disappear. Trout or just the current?

Better raise the rod to find out. A deep throb indicated paydirt.

Realizing it was hooked, the rainbow hesitated only a fraction of a second before ripping away from its lair in a big boil, waking the surface and threatening to break the fragile tippet just from sheer speed. The reel sang its unusual symphony as the fish broke clear of the surface in an uncontrolled cartwheel and tail walk toward the horizon. The heavy shouldered rainbow dove for cover and got under a weed bed. Acting quickly got the line out from the weed bed just as the trout took off downstream. There was no choice but to follow.

The Henry's Fork rainbow gradually began to tire and its runs shortened. Side pressure with the rod turned the fish toward shore, into an eddy behind a rock where the fighter finally threw in the towel. It measured 22 inches and probably weighed 4 pounds. A beautiful wild trout lay in the shallows with its side gleaming iridescent silver and crimson. The required barbless fly slipped out easily and a few seconds of reviving the trout showed it was not as tired as it seemed as it showered me with river water in a powerful surge back into the main river.

Memorable? Yes. Unusual? Not really. The Henry's Fork is one of the true Meccas of the fishing world and countless stories are told of its challenging trout, gorgeous waters and amazing countryside. Its waters are considered the epitome of trout streams. It has something for fly fishermen of all skill levels. Henry's Fork fishing can include solitude, social fishing, super-challenging trout, easy trout, float fishing, wade fishing, bank fishing, stillwater fishing, great guides and much more. The area has an interesting history, abundant wildlife, great lodging, camping, sightseeing and family activities.

Wildlife lovers are likely to see elk, deer, moose, antelope, swans, geese, sandhill cranes, eagles, osprey, kingfishers, otters, marmot and a variety of other critters. The meadows, streams and highlands are covered with flowers of many types and berries abound, when in season.

Whatever type of trout water you like to fish, the Henry's Fork is likely to have it, in abundance. Henry's Lake and Island Park Reservoir both have trophy trout possibilities for fish over 10 pounds. The river has gentle meadow waters, swift, weedy flats, riffles, rapids, runs, pools and pocket water that has produced trout to over 20 pounds. Dry fly fishing here is world famous but there are also many almost overlooked nymphing and streamer fishing opportunities.

The Henry's Fork has also gained fame from being on the forefront of fly fishing techniques and conservation. It was one of the first trout streams in the West to adopt special regulations aimed at preserving the wild trout the river harbors. Controversy over proper management and conservation of the river is ongoing and organizations like the Henry's Fork Foundation are watching, studying, improving and preserving the river for the future.

In case you heard the river is too crowded, forget it, it's not a major concern now. The river is crowded only at brief places and times. You can almost always find solitude if that appeals to you. In fact, much of the Henry's Fork is lightly fished or even under fished. Even the popular stretches are almost dovoid of pressure if your trip is timed right.

This River Journal is written from the almost 20 years of fishing experiences I've had here and from the comments of other experts on the river. The experts almost never agree on the best techniques, places to fish or conservation methods but they all love this remarkable river. Each of the guides, shop owners, local anglers, regular indigent anglers and governmental entities who have visited or manage the river can tell you some new tidbit of information that can open up a world of understanding and appreciation of the environs, history or culture of the area.

The "River Overview" takes you on a guided journey through each section of the river and describes the unique character of the stretch, how to get around and what to expect when you get there. Since lakes and reservoirs are just wide spots in a river and contribute to the overall character of the river, they will be covered as well. Each stretch of river has its own character and features that I will try to capture in writing and photography.

"Trout Habits, Techniques and Tackle" takes the angler from the where to the how and why. It covers the differences of trout habits throughout the river, how to adapt your presentation techniques to the various conditions you're likely to find and tricks that the best guides might teach you.

A section on "Fly Patterns and Hatches" is then provided so you can plan on on what to tie for the river. It is divided into three main sections: One is for the slower water sections that harbor the most selective feeders and the second section is for fast water patterns used in Box Canyon, Cardiac Canyon and so on. The last section of this chapter deals with stillwater patterns.

Since families and many anglers like to take side trips, a section on the side trips and tributary waters is provided, without which a good picture of this area is not possible.

"How To Save A River" is about the river's problems and current trends in river management. A river without friends is a river without protection. What can you do to help?

◆

Lynn Sessions guiding Bill Christensen on a section of Box Canyon, a good big fish spot.

River Overview

*T*HIS RIVER OVERVIEW IS ORGANIZED TO READ easily and can also be used as a travel reference. Fly rodders and sightseers alike will find this section interesting. It is organized to start at the headwaters and continue to the confluence, so if you are just interested in one section, you can skip to that section for its particular overview.

Henry's Lake

No discussion of the Henry's Fork River would be complete without mentioning Henry's Lake. Besides being part of the headwaters, few lakes have such a renowned reputation among fly fishermen. This lake is legendary because of its large trout and fine stillwater fishing opportunities. Seldom are these waters devoid of anglers seeking a trophy trout with fly, spin or trolling tackle. The trout average 13 to 24 inches and occasionally top 30 inches.

The cutthroat trout often top 20 inches and are the most plentiful trout due to a large stocking program located right on the lake, as much as 50 percent of the lake's trout are natural spawners. The largest trout are usually the hard fighting, rainbow/cutthroat hybrids, they are fewer in number but are highly sought after. Every year there are a few fish over 10 pounds taken and sometimes much bigger. Brook trout also occasionally reach trophy proportions (close to the 8 pound state record) and 2 to 4 pounders are regularly caught. Very few brown trout exist here.

The lake, in combination with Big Springs, constitutes the headwaters of the Henry's Fork. The lake and outlet stream are a longer piece of water than the springs but Big Springs (no fishing allowed) is the major headwater source, a point some locals like to make.

Henry's Lake itself was historically smaller and shallower but a dam was installed to increase the holding capacities and regulate water for downstream irrigation needs. Despite the increased depth, the lake is fairly shallow, averaging 12 feet deep, making it a food factory for its resident trout.

The lake is easily accessed from a number of points around its perimeter. Since it does not often lend itself to very good bank or wade fishing (except in early summer), most anglers opt for float tubes, kick boats or small boats and bass style boats. Most any craft is usable when conditions are calm but Henry's Lake is infamous for its fast moving storms that pack heavy winds. Float tubers have been known to get blown across the lake, sometimes suffering hypothermia. It is generally a safe place as long as you don't go where bad weather could get you in trouble.

The lake is easy to find because it is bordered by Highway 191/20 which runs between Idaho Falls and West Yellowstone; Highway 87, from the Madison River in Montana,

also borders one side of the lake. Public boat ramps are available at the Henry's Lake State Park (just off Highway 20) and on the back side of the lake just south of Staley Springs Lodge. Private launch sites are numerous and sometimes available to anyone for a small launch fee. Much of the perimeter of the lake is private and is ringed with the expected cabins and mountain retreats. Staley Springs and Wild Rose Ranch both have accommodations, boats for rent and launch facilities. Staley Springs was an historical fish farm, until the lake was enlarged.

Staley Springs has been popular for many years. Its crystal clear spring waters attract many trout and in turn many anglers. It's not uncommon to see 15 or 20 anglers in small boats or float tubes fishing the channel near the springs. This channel is often loaded with trout keeping cool in mid-summer.

Just south of Staley Springs is the county boat dock (near the A-frame cabin) and is a popular spot for tubers, kick boaters

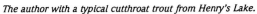

The author with a typical cutthroat trout from Henry's Lake.

Much of Henry's Lake's shoreline is private but there are a number of public and private accesses. Special regulations help preserve the fishery regardless of fishing pressure.

◆

and small boats because no launch fee is charged yet and it provides access from the Staley Springs to Kelly Creek Area. Its coves and points are all prime water for cutthroats and occasional hybrids, especially until mid-summer. Fish deeper water off the weed beds in mid-summer.

In June, mid-morning caddis hatches allow you to cast to cruising trout in shallow water. One of the few times and places where dry fly fishing can be successful on Henry's Lake.

The lake between the county boat dock (NW end) and the hatchery (NE end) is known for its hybrid fishing and also for brook trout throughout the season. Cutthroat trout are concentrated near the springs and creek mouths early in the season but are fairly well distributed most of the time.

The north shore is a popular place because of easy access from Wild Rose Ranch. Fish frequent this area (which is near the hatchery) as they prepare to spawn. Rental boats are available at Wild Rose Ranch and at Staley Springs if you don't bring a float tube.

The Stump Hole, between Staley Springs and Wild Rose Ranch, has been becoming a popular place to fish. Just park next to the road at the clearing beyond the tree-line and carry your float tube or kick boat to the water.

The Targhee Creek area on the east shore is also good during early summer and fall. Mid-summer trout fishing is generally good along shorelines only in the early morning. If the weather is hot, concentrate in the deeper water one or two hundred yards off shore.

In the SE corner of the lake is Henry's Lake State Park, a popular camping spot for boaters. It provides easy access to the Howard Creek and Outlet arm areas, which are great early season spots. Straight off the point are some weed beds that provide good fishing in mid-summer.

The south and west shores are mostly private land. One public access is located near where the outlet neck narrows. The rutted road leaves the main road on the south end of the lake between Bootjack Pass and Sawtell RV Park. The outlet area is good fishing in the early part of the season until about mid-July. An area known as "the Cliffs" on the south side of the lake near Hope and Kinney Creeks is good throughout the season and a piece of water a hundred yards north of the cliffs is a good boat fishing area.

Every year new fly patterns surface and become the popular fly for local shops to sell. They are usually some color variation of the Woolly Bugger, Maribou Leech or Yarn Leech. Black, brown, tan, peacock and red are favorite colors. Other patterns that do well here are Mickey Finns, Henry's Lake Shrimp, Prince Nymphs, Renegades, Scuds, Green Damsels, Old Faithfuls, Wiggle Bugs, Beadhead Nymphs and other tan, black or brown nymphs. If caddis are hatching, try caddis emergers and dry flies in the shallows.

Some of the best stillwater fishing I have ever seen has come from this great lake. I can recall having 80+ fish days when trout populations were at their highest. Trout numbers are not as high now but their size and growth rates are excellent. If you do anything right, you are likely to have some fine fishing. It's not uncommon to catch a dozen or more fish in a day, with several being 20 inches or better.

The Henry's Lake Foundation was formed to protect and enhance the trout fishery of Henry's Lake. This is being done by influencing budget priorities, feeder stream restoration, informing the public and creating a voice for the public. If you are interested in joining or contributing, contact Henry's Lake Foundation, 15200 NW Burlington Ct., Portland, OR 97231.

Henry's Lake is a place that can and will get into a stillwater angler's soul. Its beautiful basin and bountiful trout can really get to you.

Headwaters to Island Park Reservoir

The stream between Henry's Lake and the Big Springs confluence is a beautiful stretch of water that is heavily willow lined but flows through a large meadow known as Henry's Lake Flat. The meadow and stream is a favorite haunt for moose, sandhill cranes and pronghorn antelope as well as many birds of prey.

It has been lightly fished in the past because much of it was a private cattle ranch and access was difficult except the section from the highway to Henry's Lake Dam. Much of the

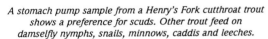

A stomach pump sample from a Henry's Fork cutthroat trout shows a preference for scuds. Other trout feed on damselfly nymphs, snails, minnows, caddis and leeches.

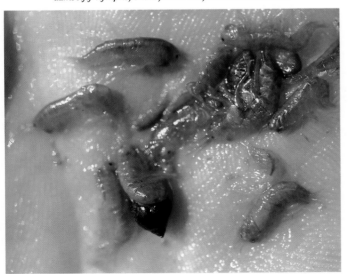

Float tubing Henry's Lake is a pleasant way to spend a day and you may catch many cutthroats, rainbows and brookies. Early summer and fall are favorite times on this prolific lake.

stream is shallow and the trout concentrate in the deeper holes. It has the potential to become a first class trout stream if river flows are moderated, simulating the spring fed flows that once existed here (before the dam). I was recently told that the Nature Conservancy has acquired much of Henry's Lake Flat, so management of this fragile ecosystem should improve. It is a piece of water to keep an eye on.

Henry's Lake Outlet meets Big Springs and then becomes the Henry's Fork at that point. The Henry's Fork was named after Andrew Henry, a trapper who came to this area in 1810. Other trappers came and they took an estimated 75,000 beaver pelts from this region between 1818 and 1840. Jim Bridger and Jedediah Smith were among them. The first white settler was Gilman Sawtell who came in 1868. Sawtell Peak was named after him. Naturally, the area was often used by the many American Indian tribes that frequented this part of the Rockies. The Shoshone, Bannock, Lemhis and Tukuarikas (Sheepeaters) all spent time in the area and other tribes such as the Blackfeet, Crow, Flathead and Nez Percé traveled through. The Henry's Fork is also known as the North Fork of the Snake River because it is one of the main tributaries of the Snake River.

Following page: Henry's Lake looking towards Reynolds Pass (to the Madison River).

11

Big Springs gushes from some rock formations at Johnny Sack's Cabin, east of Mack's Inn. It is a popular tourist attraction but no fishing is allowed in the entire stretch, down to the confluence. Some tame trout can be fed from the bridge. The confluence is known as the bathtub and is locally known for its population of trout that reside there but are hard to catch. Evening hatches always bring many fish to the surface, but try small nymphs during the day.

From the confluence downstream the Henry's Fork flows through mostly private property where bank access is limited but it is a very popular stretch of water for family float trips. The float starts at Big Springs Water Trail boat launch and goes 3 or 4 miles to the Highway 20 bridge at Mack's Inn. Make sure you don't fish until you reach the confluence with Henry's Lake Outlet. Almost any watercraft is good for this stretch. Canoes, rafts, kick boats, inner tubes and flat bottom boats are all acceptable.

Weed beds and gentle, shallow water typifies this beautiful piece of river lined with rustic cabins, many dating to the early 1900s. Most of the trout are small but some surprisingly

Crystal-clear Big Springs, at the headwaters of the Henry's Fork, is protected from fishing pressure and fish are sometimes eager to be hand fed.

◆

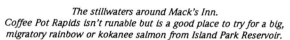

The stillwaters around Mack's Inn.
Coffee Pot Rapids isn't runable but is a good place to try for a big, migratory rainbow or kokanee salmon from Island Park Reservoir.

large fish are caught here regularly, especially in the deeper water that exists in a few spots. The historical North Fork Club is located on this stretch.

Below the bridge at Mack's Inn, the river stays a similar character but it becomes public land from the Upper Coffee Pot Campground downstream. The exclusive Flat Rock Club has been located here since about 1903. Its members are avid fly fishermen and conservationists that have influenced management of the river for a long time.

Most of this stretch is easily waded but there are a few holes near islands or log structures that you should watch out for. In late May and early June, large trout are often caught on dry flies. These fish are mostly post-spawn fish that have remained in the river instead of retreating back to Island Park Reservoir. The fish that are here mid-summer are mostly smaller resident fish and planters that are regularly stocked to provide recreation for the bait, spin and fly anglers that use this stretch.

There is a big split in opinion on how this area should be regulated. The fishing has gone downhill in recent years and many anglers want more restrictive regulations placed on the river. Others complain that some parts of the river have already been made fly fishing, catch-and-release only regulations and changing this stretch would discriminate against those who do not fly fish and who want to keep some trout.

So in the meantime, the river is stocked regularly and little is being done to study and fix the problems that exist with the fishery. One suggestion for a solution deals with mandatory release of all wild fish. Hatchery fish will be marked with a clipped dorsal fin that has healed. All trout with unclipped fins must be immediately released. This program is already underway in Idaho's steelhead fisheries, and it works well. Still, some good fishing can be had here.

In September and October, kokanee (landlocked sockeye) salmon can sometimes be seen on their spawning run out of Island Park Reservoir. Large trout often follow them up and feed on the eggs, just like Alaskan rainbows. Fall fishing is worth a try.

Floating from Mack's Inn to Upper Coffee Pot Campground is an easy but short float. Floating from the campground to Island Park Reservoir is not recommended because of a narrow, rocky cataract known as Coffee Pot Rapids. It has been floated but usually with disastrous results and lining the boat through is difficult. It is, however, a good place for a confident wader to fish some productive pocket water. It is accessed by a moderately steep hike down from several gravel and dirt access roads that take off from the Coffee Pot Road. Nearly all the holding water behind rocks in the fast water has trout that range from small resident trout to very large rainbows that have moved up from the reservoir. Nymphs, streamers, wet flies and occasionally dry flies all work here.

An unimproved trail parallels the river from the Upper Coffee Pot Campground down through the rapids. As the grade decreases and the river calms, it has a stretch with some log jams and deep holes and then it flattens out again as it approaches the top end of Island Park Reservoir. It is good streamer, dry fly and nymph water but fishing can be spotty. When the big trout are in the river it can be great. If not, you may only catch small rainbows and whitefish. Thoroughly work any water that looks like big fish holding water.

Island Park Reservoir

This large reservoir is created by a dam on the river at the top of Box Canyon. The river channel it flooded is only a few miles long but it has backed up into a long meadow valley between Thurman Ridge and Shotgun Valley and created a great fishery. It has the potential to be one of the best stillwater fisheries in the West.

Depending on the water level, the West End can be one of the best trout waters you've ever seen or it could be completely dry. This huge shallow flat is a fish factory similar to Henry's Lake. It boasts some excellent dry fly fishing in June and early July when the mayflies are hatching. It is much like the famous "gulper" hatch on Hebgen Lake in Montana. It is one place where 10 pounders have been hooked on dry flies.

The West End is spring fed and rich in aquatic life. It is often excellent leech, streamer and nymph water. You never know if the next fish is going to be 10 inches or 10 pounds. I've had large trout straighten size 6 hooks or break 1X tippet on the strike. Their strength can be compared to the famous Henry's Lake hybrids (for naturalized holdovers). It was drained dry in 1992 but is coming back very well as of the 1994 season. The next few years should see some excellent fishing as long as water levels can be moderated.

◆

Trout rising on the upper end of Island Park Reservoir with Sawtell Peak shrouded in a summer rain cloud.
A silent sentinel near the Montana border.

A nice wild rainbow from Box Canyon.

◆

Island Park Reservoir, like many of the Henry's Fork waters, has had its share of controversial management decisions. It was poisoned in 1979 and again in 1992 to remove undesirable species. Both times the lake was almost completely drained to make it easier to rotenone. Both times, it flushed huge amounts of silt into the river below as the exposed river channel dug through years of accumulated sediments to reach its original bed. It was estimated that 50,000 tons of sediment was flushed out in 1992, which impacted the fishery downstream in many ways. The river below the dam was also completely dried up with the exception of some small springs and the water supplied by the Buffalo River, which enters the Henry's Fork just below the dam. Without this water, the river would likely have been killed for quite a distance.

The silt from the draining reservoir filled up many of the holes that existed in the slower sections of the river, such as Harriman State Park. Some thought it was taps for the river. Luckily it was not. High flows shortly afterwards flushed out much of the silt but it also scoured the river. Thousands of trout that were flushed out with the reservoir water gave the trout populations in the river a boost. The 1993 season was one of the best for big trout in recent times. But remember that this was an artificial situation, not a quick rebound for the river.

The dam has been worked on almost every year, which usually calls for a big drawdown and a new power structure was recently added to the dam to capture the river's energy. Hopefully they are through playing with the dam for a while so the rebounding fishery in the reservoir will have a chance.

An access point for the reservoir is located at Island Park Dam. The bays and fingers near the dam are best in June. The trout are also sometimes concentrated in the main lake body when the water is low.

The West End is the best fly fishing spot and remains ideal fly rod water until low water levels dry it up. It is accessed by taking the Green Canyon Road (at Harriman State Park's main exit) up over scenic Green Canyon Pass to an area known as "the Fingers." Dozens of these fingers, some meadowlike and others wooded, reach out into the lake from Thurman Ridge. There is a campground (West End) and boat ramp and many places for float tubers and kick boaters to access the water.

Box Canyon

If I had to choose one section of river that has been my best and most consistent producer, it would have to be Box Canyon. When I guided the river, it was my specialty and I always have to hit it regardless of the other river sections I fish. It has a deserved reputation for eating anglers. Few anglers that fish it regularly have not been properly baptized. It is a shallow box-like canyon about 4 miles long that is full of rapids, pocket water, swift, rocky flats and fast, boulder-filled runs. The canyon rim is heavily wooded and harbors many osprey, marmot, occasional bald eagles and moose.

Unless you consider yourself an aggressive and skilled wader, you'd best not attempt this stretch without a drift boat and preferably a guide. Any skilled oarsman can run the Box Canyon in a raft, drift boat or larger kick boat but you must keep on your toes to avoid the many rocks and occasional sweepers.

Many excellent guides work the river. They are mostly very experienced and well trained. If you want a guided trip, even at the last minute, call Lynn Sessions at Last Chance Lodge and Outfitters or Mike Lawson at Henry's Fork Anglers and they should be able to set a trip up for you. They also keep track of where the best fishing is located and can show you the best techniques so you don't spend your whole vacation fumbling with improper flies and methods.

While you can catch fish drift fishing Box Canyon with big dry flies or streamers, it's usually best to anchor up or pull over and wade in good looking runs or channels and thoroughly fish these areas with big nymphs. Weighted Rubber-Leg Stoneflies and Prince Nymphs are old standbys. Woolly Buggers, Sculpins, Hare's Ears, San Juan Worms, Glow Bugs, Wiggle Bugs, Trudes, and salmonfly adult imitations are also worth trying. Small flies are seldom very effective here but there are exceptions.

The top end of "the Box," right below Island Park Dam, is a varied piece of water that often provides some good dry fly fishing in addition to nymphing and streamer fishing. My friend Bob Johnson caught a 28 inch beauty on a size 16 caddis dry a couple years ago. It's not uncommon to catch 14-22 inchers mixed in with the smaller rainbows. I had one day where I hooked and landed two, thick 24 inchers on consecutive casts here. I took my rod apart and quit for the day with a big grin

◆

Mike Lawson is one of those rare individuals whose identity has become associated with the river, not just because of his fly shop, or because he guides lots of people, but because he has become a deciding factor in the positive future of this remarkable fishery.

The dory lineup at Henry's Fork Anglers Fly Shop. Using one of the guide services in the area is a great way to get to know the water.

◆

on my face. It is also the only piece of the Box where an unsure wader can find some water to fish relatively unscathed.

The outlet hole at the dam is deep and full of big rocks and big trout. You'll also catch some occasional big suckers. It is fished fairly hard and the trout don't always come easy but there are some 6-12 pounders here that reward patience and proper technique.

Just below this hole is a mid-stream gravel bar. It is best accessed from the far side of the dam (not the boat ramp side, except during low water). Both sides provide excellent nymphing and the heavily wooded side has some very good dry fly water.

The boat ramp for Box Canyon is located here and is accessed by taking the Island Park Dam road (just north of Pond's Lodge) and turning left just before you reach the dam. If you float the river, shuttles are available from Last Chance Lodge & Outfitters at Last Chance, the small community at the bottom end of your float along Highway 20.

The long run extending downstream from the launch ramp is well known for its big trout. It's swift but fairly easy wading here, but the lower end is deep as the river backs up for the first rapids at the mouth of the Buffalo River. There are often rainbows and small brook trout rising just above the rapids.

The following chute is quite fast but anywhere there are small pockets of holding water, there are usually trout. If you are not used to fishing such fast water, you might be intimidated at first and think that no trout could hold in that current. Remember that there are many rocks along the bottom that provide good cover and feeding lies for trout. Use enough weight to get your nymphs and streamers down. If you're not losing flies, you're not fishing deep enough.

Near Box Canyon Campground (up above the canyon rim), is Will's Run, named after Will Godfrey because it was his favorite piece of big fish water. Fish deep and imagine a big trout holding behind each rock and at the bottom of the channels and you might be surprised by a big, deep bodied trout. A client caught a trout here that was only 22 1/2 inches long but weighed 7 3/4 pounds, a true "hog."

The river slows somewhat but is still fast and full of rocks. Just above a grassy bank section called "the Meadows" is a couple deep troughs that hold many big trout for the angler that can handle the challenging wading and tricky currents behind big boulders. Fishing from an anchored boat or while a guide holds the boat in position is the best way to fish this stretch since it occasionally eats even the best of waders. The river widens out at the Meadows and can be good dry fly water using big attractors. At low water a good wader can criss-cross this section covering the water with dries or streamers.

After this long, flat stretch, the river makes a bend to the left and the rapids here create a wonderful run for good sized trout and huge whitefish. Nymphing is best here but also try streamers. If you wade it, use a wading staff for support. A careful nympher can spend a whole day in this one hundred yard stretch, if his or her legs survive.

A couple hundred yards downstream is an access point known as the falls run. Just below the access road, and on the far canyon wall is a small waterfall. This whole stretch is good nymphing, streamer and dry fly water. If you climb down the canyon wall here, be careful. A rim trail gives access to the stretches of water above and below but there are only a few safe trails to get down to the river.

Most of the river from here down is potential holding water and there is one more road access to the river before you get to the cabins at the mouth of the river. Look for groups of rocks out in the current and channels that are just slightly deeper than the rest of the river. The water is often greenish and the rocks are dark green with the deeper channels looking lighter green in color. Concentrate on deeper channels and the water where rapids spill into deeper water.

Here again, the careful nympher or systematic streamer fisherman can do very well. Fall fishing this stretch can be incredible. Below the last access road but above the first cabin is a very good run that is often overlooked. It is full of good sized trout that average 14-22 inches but sometimes get much bigger.

The bottom end of this run turns into rapids that plunge into a beautiful hole at the first cabins. The largest Box Canyon trout landed in recent years came from this hole. It was a huge 18 pounder caught by a local named Ron Dye. Trout of this size still exist but are rarely caught, and landed even less often.

The canyon opens up here and provides some good dry fly water. Fish trudes or hoppers mid-day and caddis in the evenings. This section can be wade fished by crossing the river below the last cabin and fishing up the far bank. The evening

◆

Kurt Barker shows how the most successful guides fish their clients. Walking the boat through good water allows clients to fish the better runs of Box Canyon with nymphs and streamers.

A good friend, Mark Smith (one of the excellent guides on the river) and his bride Glenna just before their riverside wedding. Those who make their livelihood from the river often do so not so much for a good living but for the love of the river and its lifestyle.

hatches can bring up some big trout. The wading is still pretty tough but most people can attempt it with a wading staff. The take out for the Box Canyon float is here, a short distance below the last cabin.

This open area above the Harriman State Park boundaries is known as Last Chance. It is swift but flat water, with a few boulders. Wading is considerably easier here and access from the highway is easy and abundant. This is where many anglers concentrate during the famous green drake hatch of late June. The small Western drake hatches off shortly afterwards (see section on hatches and fly patterns page 41-43) and many other hatches are found here.

Harriman State Park: The Ranch

No piece of Henry's Fork water captures the imagination of a large number of anglers more than "the ranch." Once commonly called "the Railroad Ranch," it was given to the state by the Harrimans in 1977 and is now called Harriman State Park. The gift had conditions attached. It was to be managed so there was harmony between man and wildlife. Fishing would be allowed but only after the birds had completed nesting, which is why the ranch is closed until mid-June.

It has been written about by many outdoor writers and it is legendary. Its hatches can be so prolific that one wonders how the fish could ever find your fly in the continous raft of living and spent aquatic and terrestrial insects. Perhaps its challenging fishing has also created a lure for experienced anglers wanting to test their mettle against some of the most selective trout anywhere. Some of the fly fishing techniques and fly patterns used all over the world were originally perfected here. Inexperienced anglers figure that if they can learn to catch trout here, they can catch fish anywhere but it can even frustrate experts at times.

At first glance, the river looks sluggish and flat but a million currents, from fast to still, tear at attempts to get a drag-free drift. The weed beds, rocks and substrate variances all enter into the factoring. The trout has many food choices and even when you are able to imitate their foods exactly, they often frustrate you by feeding in a rhythm all their own or by cruising as they feed, not coming up at the same place twice. This piece of water has many subtle clues to trout feeding activity and is a game of finesse, not the masculine tromping that Box Canyon anglers endure.

The upper ranch is all meadow-like. From the upper ranch parking lot, a trail follows the bank all the way down the river. This is a classic meadow spring creek but one of the biggest spring creeks you'll ever see. From the Last Chance area, the ranch angles westward and then into a big horseshoe bend and an island area known as bonefish flats. It was named this because the preferred method of fishing here is stalking trout that are feeding, much like bonefish anglers do except that trout don't move as much. They are very spooky and improper wading and sloppy casts can put them down for a while. How you present the fly is very critical. One nice aspect of hunting

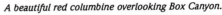

A beautiful red columbine overlooking Box Canyon.

This beautiful sunset on Harriman State Park was caused by fires in the SW corner of Yellowstone Park. Commonly called the "Ranch", this stretch of water has been written about extensively in angling literature and has reached legendary status.

Millionaires Pool and many islands mark the lower half of the upper ranch. Access is available by paying a small day use fee at the park headquarters just west of Osborne Bridge (Highway 20) on Green Mountain Road. A tour of the ranch facilities is quite interesting if the fishing is slow. Two parking areas give access to the river where it bends back towards the highway. Much of this area is wooded, rather than meadow, and is very scenic. Each bend and twist in the river has its own character. Some deep holes suggest cautious wading. Once you get to know the water, you can wade many places but until you do, be cautious. The easy wading can lead to a false sense of security, watch where others are wading.

The river just above Osborne Bridge breaks character and becomes a sprawling riffle full of rocks. The water at the base is often the scene for prolific caddis hatches in the evening. The deep water right by the bridge also holds some large trout.

Despite losing a couple years worth of young trout to river problems, there are a good number of 10-12 inchers, lots of 4-5 inchers and many fry. Spawning success has been great lately. Most of the bigger trout are in the 15-22 inch range. Because of the reservoir drawdown mentioned earlier, there are a fair number of reservoir trout in the ranch. They were easy to catch in 1993 because they were not conditioned to anglers yet but in 1994 they began to feed much like the resident fish and got harder to fool. Still, they generally do not fight quite as hard as the resident fish and most anglers would rather see wild trout than lots of dumb hatchery fish with poor genetics.

Anglers can bankfish (in a few spots), wade and float the ranch. If you float, put in at the Last Chance area and take out at Osborne Bridge. Fishing from a boat is not very productive for the most part so float until you spot some risers then anchor the boat in the middle of the river and get out to stalk the ris-

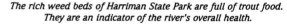

The rich weed beds of Harriman State Park are full of trout food. They are an indicator of the river's overall health.

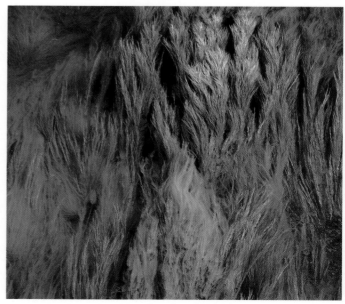

trout is that you can catch all big trout, because you don't cast to the splashy rises of smaller trout or whitefish.

Another access called "the mailbox" is in the middle of the upper ranch. You can park opposite the park boundary where an old road, gate and big wood mailbox still exist from days gone by. It is a good hike in but often can get you away from the crowds (if they exist). A bridge and some broken water causes deeper water. Most of the ranch is wadable but there is just enough deep water that you must be very careful while wading. A wading staff is valuable to probe the weedy bottom ahead of you to make sure it is not too deep or soft.

Much of the ranch has a shallow, firm middle and the edges near the bank are deeper and muddy. The bigger trout are often bank feeders that sip edibles just a few inches from shore or weed beds. An angler seldom does well in the ranch by casting blind. You are hunting trout here. Some anglers never wet a line until they see a good riser. When a big emergence is going on, there are often a half dozen or more trout rising within casting range. Don't just cast to the general area, pick a specific trout and cast directly upstream of the riseform.

Previous page: The lower "Ranch" has wide, wadable waters and big, selective trout.

Mike Lawson casts to a large weedline feeder on the Harriman State Park near the "Ranch" buildings.
Success requires that you hunt individual fish rather than just casting blind.

◆

ing trout. Make sure you respect other anglers water and don't float anywhere where you might put their fish down. If the ranch is crowded, you probably should not float because it will cause too many conflicts. Most crafts are suitable for the ranch.

The lower ranch (Osborne Bridge to Wood Road 16) is not fished as much as the upper ranch. It is quiet water with a moderate current and a deep channel runs down the middle, making it difficult to cross anywhere. Evening spinner falls, caddis hatches and brown drake hatches often make this a great stretch for evening fishing. I often fish Box Canyon or Henry's Lake during the day and then go to the lower ranch for the evening.

Access this area from the old Mesa Falls Scenic Drive. Pull off toward the river at the old gravel pits or on Wood Road 16. Across the river from Wood Road 16 is the cabin community of Pinehaven. This whole stretch is known for its big, difficult trout. This is the lower boundary of the Park and from here on down is a gradual transition to a more canyon-like scene. The river sometimes seems like it's devoid of trout until a hatch brings the trout to the surface.

Some anglers put a boat in at Osborne Bridge and float down to Riverside Campground. The boat helps you access water on the lower ranch that is seldom fished. The faster water below can be nymph fished with attractors, nymphs or

with dry flies. As with most of the Henry's Fork, it's not a bad idea to try streamers or leeches if no surface action presents itself.

Cardiac Canyon

As the river begins to cut its way through the plateau toward lower elevations, it picks up considerable speed and roughness. Access is limited to a few old logging roads and sometimes requires a hike. It can be floated but the oarsman must be competent at maneuvering through numerous rocks in fast water. This is a scenic and wild section of water that sees few anglers in a year. If you want to get away from it all, this might be your place.

Depending on who you talk to, Cardiac Canyon refers to the whole canyon from Pinehaven to the mouth of the Warm River or it refers just to the river between Upper and Lower Mesa Falls. Since the canyon is full of fast, difficult to wade, stressful water, I refer to the whole canyon as Cardiac Canyon.

The upper part of the canyon can be floated by putting in at Riverside Campground and taking out at Hatchery Ford, the only two ramps on the entire stretch. Make sure you don't miss

Following page: A rainbow caused by spray from the 112-foot Upper Mesa Falls in Cardiac Canyon.

A solitary angler braves the treacherous waters of Cardiac Canyon, just below Upper Mesa Falls.

Hatchery Ford because there are no other takeouts and three violent falls downstream. You may want to hire a guide the first time you float it. This float is seldom done because of the difficulty of the shuttle and because the fishing can be spotty.

There are concentrations of fish but other areas that appear to be devoid of fish. It is popular with a few locals during the stonefly hatch because it will bring up the bigger trout. Attractor flies and streamers are used in addition to more accurate imitations during the hatches.

From Hatchery Ford downstream, access is limited. An old road goes down to the river at Sheep Falls, and here again, the only time you're likely to see other anglers is during the stonefly hatch, shortly after the season opens. It takes off Highway 20 south of the Riverside Campground turnoff.

The next access to the river is at Upper and Lower Mesa Falls (Highway 47). It's probably not a good idea to fish above Upper Mesa Falls, a few people have gone over the 112 foot drop in years past. The falls are a big tourist attraction and you should see them even if you don't fish this area. A huge new steel and wood walkway makes viewing easy but seems like government overkill.

If you look over the rail at the river below the Upper Falls, you will see a piece of river that looks like a wader's nightmare, but there are lots of trout here. Don't even think of attempting this stressful canyon unless you are extremely confident in your physical condition and wading prowess. Even if you're the best wader in the world, take a wading staff.

There is a steep trail (climb) down into the canyon from a gate that was installed in the new railing. If the trail is too much for you, don't even try the river. Once you work your way down to the water, you will wonder where to fish because everything looks like white water. Just remember that there is a fish behind every rock and you will know where to fish because there are thousands of rocks and shelves that break the current a little.

I like to use 1X tippet, a big stonefly nymph and a strike indicator placed 4 feet from the fly. Use a short line and pop the fly into all pockets behind rocks. The trout are not selective and will hammer the fly hard. I usually keep one hand on my rod and one on my wading staff. To land the trout, I just tuck the staff under one arm. Keep the wading staff secure, you don't want to lose it. Attractor dry fly fishing is also productive at low water.

Most of the trout are 8-16 inches but there are a few trout to 22 inches as well. I work my way down to an island just downstream a quarter mile and work back and forth upstream, against the current, testing each pocket behind rocks. If the water is up, don't fish anywhere but along shore. It's possible to catch 100 fish in a day here but you might need a week to recover afterwards.

The canyon below Lower Mesa Falls is commonly called Bear Gulch. It is one of those crazy places where macho anglers go because of its difficulty of access. An access road near Grandview Campground takes you to a dead end at the rim of the canyon. Believe it or not, this is the launch ramp. You will notice that the river is still out of sight about a half mile down

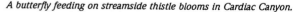

A butterfly feeding on streamside thistle blooms in Cardiac Canyon.

Frank Amato fishing near Warm River Springs.

◆

in the canyon. Some hearty anglers hike down and fish back up toward the lower falls. Others actually dump their boat here then alternately push it and get dragged down the mountain by it until they reach the river. Now I know it sounds crazy but it is done with surprising frequency. Drift boats should be tough and light and rafts should be good quality with a rowing frame. Large kick boats with oars work but don't take any other type of craft. If it survives the launch trail, it might get eaten by the river.

The river is full of rocks and rapids and there is also one small (6 foot) falls that must be navigated not too far below the put in (use the chute toward the right bank). Dry fly fishing is often fast and furious for smaller trout. Try streamers and stone-fly nymphs for larger trout. Fish of over 10 pounds have come from here but the average fish is 6-14 inches. It is not a piece of river for floating every day but makes a memorable adventure, if that is what you're after. You may see moose or a bear. As the river canyon opens up, the Warm River enters from the left. The take out is at the bridge across the Henry's Fork just below the confluence.

I only floated this stretch once, with my friend Dave Young from St. Anthony, but I dream about doing it again just for the adventure of it all. I also cannot help but think that there is a 20 pounder waiting there for me.

Warm River to Ashton

You have now reached the valley where spud and wheat farms abound on the benches but the river still flows through a scenic canyon, though not nearly as rough as Cardiac Canyon. A gravel road parallels the north side of the river much of the way down to Highway 20. An old railroad right of way on the south side of the river allows bicycle access to that side. The river can be waded in a number of access spots but floating is the most popular way to fish. The Warm River to Ashton Reservoir float is popular for guide services and a few locals, but few others fish here. Most anglers are headed to the more famous parts upstream. Their loss.

Mid-summer fishing can be good for rainbow trout, brown trout and whitefish. From here down, browns are doing fairly well. They have been in the river a long time but are now making a gradual comeback. The biggest Henry's Fork trout I have heard of was a 26 pound brown that came from the river above Ashton Reservoir a number of years ago. From Riverside to St. Anthony, special regulations (slot limits) have begun to help trout populations recover from years of drought and overharvesting of the bigger trout.

The river here has gentle and fast flows, riffles, deep holes and long runs. A couple rapids require caution but most of the float is easily accomplished in a drift boat, raft or larger kick boat. There are interesting rock formations in the canyon and occasional log jams to watch for. Many of the trout are in the deeper, swifter runs and shelves and along the banks. Casting to the banks with dry flies can be productive but nymphing with Prince Nymphs, G.R. Hare's Ears, Golden Stones, etc. often outproduces dries for larger fish. The biggest trout are caught on big, dark Leeches, Sculpins and Wiggle Bugs.

Looking upstream from the highway bridge at Ashton shows the wonderful character of the Henry's Fork.

Evening caddis hatches are often worth waiting for and wading above the Highway 20 bridge is popular.

When you get to the Highway 20 bridge, your float is almost over. The pullout is just downstream to the right. This slow backwater of the reservoir can be great fishing for cruising pods of trout in the evening. Fishing late often gets you a chance at bigger trout.

Few fly fishermen fish Ashton Reservoir but there are some very big trout here. The action may not be fast but the rewards could be great.

Ashton to Chester

Below Ashton Reservoir is some delightful dryfly and nymph water that can be easily floated in anything from a float tube to a drift boat. Much of the shoreline is private land so floating is popular. The river below the dam is open year-round to fishing and can have some good spring, early summer and fall fishing. To get here, take the main "T" in Ashton and head straight west. To fish right below the dam, cross the bridge and take the first gravel road to the right. There is a small parking area next to a couple trees and a trail down to the river. When the river is low, much of this water is wadable. It's good dry fly water.

The floating put in is accessed on the east side of the river, just below the bridge, down a gravel road. The river flows

Facing page: Lower Mesa Falls. The canyon below is one of the most adventurous floats on the river, with a steep 1/2-mile-long ramp (muscle powered) and lots of rough water including a 6 foot shelf drop.

through farm land but much of it is hidden from the river level. It is typified by long mossy runs broken by a few deep runs and occasional island channels. Wading is generally easy but watch out for knee high rocks that are almost invisible. The bigger trout are found in channels, in the deeper water but hatches often bring them into shore or to the surface in the middle of the channels.

If you see small muddy streams flowing into the river, fish the other side. These streams are usually runoff from over-irrigation and the warm water and pesticides are undesirable to trout. The fish tend to pod up in places so you want to fish the pods of rising fish thoroughly. June has an amazing gray drake hatch that brings trout up everywhere. Caddis hatches are daily occurrances and some mayflies are available, including green drakes.

The river flows under Vernon Bridge where one of the take-outs is located. Good wade fishing is available above and below the bridge. It makes a good short float, or you can continue down to Seely's Ranch take-out/put-in, just above Chester Backwaters, or to the bottom of the backwaters.

The backwaters are well known for their pods of big trout that rise mid-day on cloudy days and just about any evening or hatch. The backwaters have current throughout but it gets much too deep to wade and private property precludes walking the banks. The best way to fish it is to drift down or row upstream and drift down. Selective trout know what boats sound like so you should be as quiet as possible and expect to make long, accurate casts. If you can anchor near pods of working fish without putting them down, all the better.

Fish these backwater fish as you might fish Harriman State

Unusual rock formations that can only be seen by floating the river below the Warm River access.

◆

Park fish, by stalking them (from the boat) and presenting the fly down-and-across with plenty of slack for a drag-free float. Try nymphs with a strike indicator on a long leader or leeches if fish are not rising. Work them in the channels between weed beds. The absolute end of this float is at the dam. Don't get washed over, the hydraulics could trap you there. The Falls River comes into the backwaters just above the take-out, on the left bank. You can access this spot by taking the Chester turnoff on Highway 20 and driving west, through the 4-way stop and continuing until you see a Chester Dam access sign and turning right there.

Chester to St. Anthony

Just below Chester Dam is a beautiful riffle full of small trout, with a few big ones mixed in for fun. Much of it is wadable during low water and a whole day can be spent within sight of the dam. A boat can also be put in here and a float made to St. Anthony, at the old Fun Farm Bridge sportsman's access. The numbers of trout are good with most being 8 to 14 inches in length. Fifteen to twenty four inchers, while not common, are available.

This is a gentle float over a gravel bottom with occasional ledge drop-offs, islands and deeper runs. It can have prolific hatches of caddis and other insects, plus leech patterns often

move some bigger trout. It is a fairly short float but can last all day by getting out and wading any good looking water.

As you approach the pull-out bridge, the current goes slack and another almost stillwater situation is formed. Evening hatches can bring up numerous trout and cloudy, unsettled weather can make dry fly fishing good all day long. If sunny conditions persist, fish the riffles and deep pockets near fast water for best success.

The Lower River

From St. Anthony downstream there is about 20 miles of what could be prime trout water. The river is lightly fished because of private property, many small diversion structures that make floating difficult and because of dewatering problems. Yet despite its problems, there can be good fishing in the areas where water remains during summer irrigation demands.

Even many of the canals have good trout fishing, attesting to the damage that canals can inflict to trout populations. Every summer, trout end up in the canals and every fall, when the canals are dried up, thousands of trout lose their lives. Despite the river's ability to come back, no piece of trout river can stand to yearly dewaterings. It is even lawful to pitchfork trout out of the drying canals at the end of the irrigation season.

I have heard of people who jet boat the lower part of the river and have found trout to 6 pounds, so despite its problems,

◆

Watercraft for the Henry's Fork is varied. Drift boats are the old standby but kick boats such as this are gaining popularity. (Pictured here is Lynn Sessions of Last Chance Outfitters)

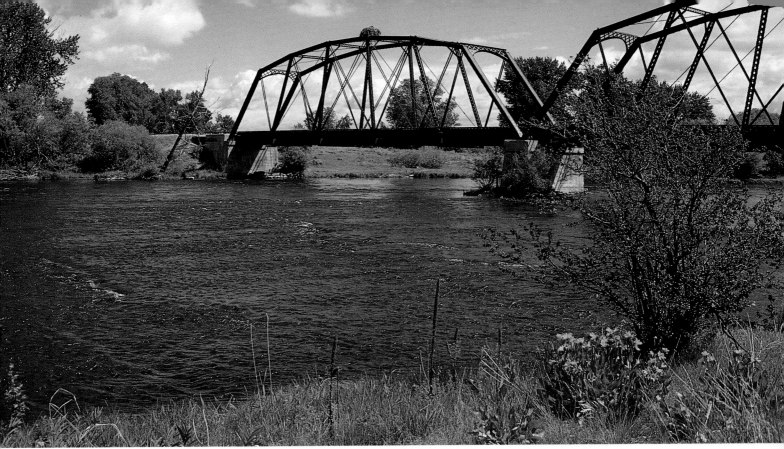

An old railroad bridge near St. Anthony shows that the river has great potential if water users don't dry it up every summer. An osprey nest overlooks the river.

there are still sections of river below St. Anthony that keep a population of trout. Some of the trout make it back to the river when the canals are drained and some springs give trout habitat. I'd really like to see fish screens on the canals and a minimum flow kept in the river year-round.

The dewatering problems seem too severe for now but hopefully there will be a time when irrigation and wildlife needs can be balanced. I hope that will happen because it is an incredibly beautiful section of river with many braided chanels, riffles, spring creeks and backwaters.

The Henry's Fork has its share of problems, which we will touch on again in the final chapter, but it continues to draw anglers from around the world and its future looks bright. If you have been to the Henry's Fork before, you should visit it again and if you have never been here, please invite yourself to sample its wonderful variety of fishing. I'd love to have the river for myself but a river without friends is a river that's in trouble.

Who to Contact

*American Adventures Association, P.O. Box 8171, Salt Lake City, UT 84108. Ph. 801-484-5924. (Quality Henry's Fork Maps).

*BS (Bill Scheiss) Flies, HC 66 Box 187, Island Park, ID 83429. Ph. 208-558-7879. (Henry's Lake Guide, Flies).

*Charleston Books, 470 South 1300 East, Salt Lake City, Utah 84102. (Novel, *Snake River Country* by Sid Eliason, based in Henry's Fork area).

*Elk Creek Station, Ph. 208-558-7271. (Gas, groceries, repairs).

*Forest Service Recreation Reservations, Ph. 1-800-280-CAMP (Area Forest Service campgrounds).

*Henry's Fork Anglers, Inc., HC 66, Box 491, Island Park, ID 83429. Ph. (summer) 208-558-7525, (winter) 208-624-3590. (Fly shop, guide service, fly fishing schools, fishing info.).

*Henry's Fork Foundation, Inc., P.O. Box 61, Island Park, ID 83429. Ph. 208-558-9041. (Organization to protect Henry's Fork).

*Henry's Fork Landing, Ph. 208-558-7672. (Cafe, store, floats).

*Henry's Fork Lodge, HC 66 Box 600, Island Park, ID 83429. Ph. 208-558-7953. (Lodging, restaurant, guide service).

*Island Park Village Resort, Ph. 208-558-7502. (Condos, golf, dining, dancing).

*Lakeside Lodge/Campground, P.O. Box 316, Island Park, ID 83429. Ph. 208-558-7147. (Lodging, restaurant, store).

*Last Chance General Store, Ph. 208-558-7399. (Gas, store, tackle).

*Last Chance Lodge & Outfitters, HC 66, Box 482, Island Park, ID 83429. Ph. 1-800-428-8338. (Lodging, fly shop, guide services, shuttles, fishing info.).

*Lucky Dog Retreat, P.O. Box 128, Island Park, ID 83429. Ph. 208-558-7455. (Rustic lodging, dinners).

*Mack's Inn, 208-558-7272. (Lodging, R.V. park, floats, miniature golf, plays).

*Pond's Lodge, P.O. Box 258, Island Park, ID 83429. Ph. 208-558-7221. (Lodging, restaurant, bar, store).

One of many wildflowers found around Henry's Fork.

———————————————◆———————————————

*Sawtelle Mountain Resort, Ph. 1-800-574-0404. (Lodging, camping, dinners, horse/bike rentals).
*Shotgun General Store & Cafe, Ph. 208-558-7090. (Store, gas, showers).
*Staley Springs Lodge (Henry's Lake), HC 66, Box 102, Island Park, ID 83429. Ph. 208-558-7471. (Lodging, boat rentals).
*Three Rivers Ranch, Box 856, Ashton, ID 83420. Ph. 208-652-3750. (Lodge, guide service).

Trout Habits, Techniques and Tackle

Now that you know a little about the different sections of the river, lets get into some technical understanding of the trout. This section helps you sort out the differences in trout habits throughout the river and will give some basic instructions on how to fish the flies you will be using. The text assumes that you already know how to cast, and know some basic fly fishing techniques and knots. To understand fishing in the various sections of river one must first understand that there are several colonies or classes of trout, each with their own habits, food preferences and idiosyncrasies. Understanding strike zones, perception factors, imprinting, fly drift level etc. will increase your understanding of trout behavior and will help you catch more trout.

Trout Classes

Trout are not intelligent animals but they do have marvelous instincts and the ability to act quickly on small amounts of information. Although we may try to adhere human characteristics and intelligence to them, they are not smart, but they are naturally wiley. They are not malicious, but they are cautious. No two areas of a river are alike and because a trout's survival instinct is strong, they adapt to the conditions with which they find themselves associated. Each fish develops different habits through environmental conditioning.

Think about the differences between Aborigines, Asians, Europeans and Central Americans. We are of the same species but all have different customs, eating habits, sizes and preferred locations. It is because we also have a strong survival instinct and adapt to the situation we find ourselves placed in. In that way we are like trout.

A trout's brain is about the size of a pea. Hopefully ours is much bigger but because a trout has such good instincts and fast reactions, it helps make up for a lack of pure intelligence. What often looks to us like extremely educated, selective behavior is really just a trout's ability to key in on one or two aspects of their foods and then act quickly on that small amount of information. A trout cannot analyze the whole makeup of the fly, the intricacies of your presentation and the expense of your equipment. The trout instead will key in on an insect's wings, legs, surface impression or its float, though not all these things at once.

For example: If a pale morning dun is hatching, the upright, creamy white wings are not only distinctive but are the first thing that enters the trout's cone of vision. Because of this, the wing can get imprinted on a trout's mind through conditioned response and become its feeding trigger. Trout may ignore everything else but that wing silhouette. So if your fly does not have a good wing silhouette, it will be totally ignored. Other trout see a surface impression and it is often combined

———————————————◆———————————————

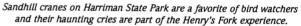
Sandhill cranes on Harriman State Park are a favorite of bird watchers and their haunting cries are part of the Henry's Fork experience.

A Box Canyon trout on a stonefly nymph. The Henry's Fork strain of wild rainbows are a hybrid cutthroat known for its fighting prowess. Wild fish that spawn naturally are considered superior sportfish to the genetically inferior hatchery planters that most fish and game agencies introduce to fisheries today.

with natural drift because the surface impression does not look right if the fly is dragging in the surface film.

Selective nymphing trout often key in on the size or shape of the naturals and anything that does not fit those parameters will be rejected. There are several classes of trout behavior seen regularly on the Henry's Fork, they relate to trout anywhere but will help you decide what type of fly and presentation technique is neccessary.

There are basically three types of trout habits that are easily recognizable. The first is uneducated trout. These are trout that have not seen humans, ever or in a while, and do not get fished over regularly. They are generally easy to catch, sometimes stunted and often quite spooky. If a bird flies over or they see you, they will dive for cover. Most food that comes by is worth a try, which makes big attractor flies a first choice because of their visibility. Many of the trout in Cardiac Canyon and some in Henry's Lake Outlet are this way. Some reservoir trout also seldom see people.

The second class of trout is educated trout. These are trout that have been fished over regularly and where release of fish is not mandatory so the "dumb" fish might get harvested. The fish that are left can be wiley. They don't just come easily to any fly. You must imitate what they are feeding on predominantly or attract them with a proper attractor pattern, usually smaller in size. One of the first things that selective trout do is go to smaller but abundant foods, they are generally safer to eat and few anglers fish them properly. Presentation becomes important because trout reject unnatural looking drifts and

oversize flies. Use small flies in slow water and larger, but good, imitations in fast water. Trout feed at certain times of day and then selectively. Opportunistic feeding is limited but still present. Henry's Fork fish that show these tendencies are located above Island Park Reservoir (including Henry's Lake) and from Warm River to St. Anthony.

The third class of trout habits is the most interesting. I call these fish "educated catch-and-release trout." In the past there were few of these waters, until the late 70s, but many trout waters today have catch-and-release regulations (slot limits included). The trout actually get conditioned to the presence of humans and accept them as a natural part of its environment. There are periods when angler density is so great that if trout quit feeding everytime an angler is detected, they could very well starve to death. Their survival instinct won't let them do that. Accordingly, the trout learn to feed even when a human presence is near. They may get more selective but they continue to feed.

Each trout develops a different way to deal with the pressure. Some only feed during hatches, some feed mainly on nymphs and seldom rise, some feed only during low light periods, some are very drag sensitive and will not take a fly with the least bit of drag. Other trout key in on the fly's size, surface impression or occasionally color. Like I mentioned before, the trout key in on one or two aspects of their foods and ignore

Following page: Box Canyon is a great fishery for those who like big trout in fast water. Tough wading makes many anglers opt for a float trip.

Moose, such as this one near the historic Flat Rock Club, are a common sight along the river.

"matching the hatch" is often the best way to go, you must assume that a fish is feeding on one specific food or you might be force feeding it something it does not want. Attractors use many other triggers to help catch trout, not just hunger.

I obviously cannot describe all the techniques that can be used on the Henry's Fork trout so I will describe some of the most effective ones and the tackle that's used for each.

Down-and-Across Presentation

This dry fly, terrestrial and emerger technique was perfected on the Henry's Fork because the traditional up-and-across presentation often fails. It allows the angler to present the fly to fish that are feeding along the bank or weed beds so the fly reaches the fish before the leader and line is seen. It's especially useful on the flat water of Harriman State Park and Chester Backwaters.

The angler wades carefully to a point that is across or up and across from the rising fish they're stalking. The cast is made across or down-and-across to a point several feet above the fish. The drift lane is often critical because a trout will often not move more than 2 or 3 inches to either side to feed. On windy days, it helps to make the cast past the feeding lane, the rod can then be raised smoothly, dragging the fly into the proper drift lane. As soon as the fly reaches the proper drift lane, drop the rod tip and give it enough slack to float over the trout without any drag. When it passes, gently swing the fly away from the fish and pick up the line for another cast. Don't false cast over the trout or you may put it down.

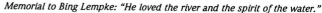

Memorial to Bing Lempke: "He loved the river and the spirit of the water."

most other things, which is why most trout don't really see the hook.

One interesting thing is that even very selective trout can often be taken on attractors or other hatch busters such as terrestrial insects. Attractors are often taken because of curiosity, or perhaps they are bored with the present hatch. Big attractors seldom do well except in fast water but small ones often catch the fish's eye and trigger a feeding response.

The trigger can be the imprint that is on the trout's mind. If it still has a faded imprint from a previous hatch on its mind, a certain attractor pattern with a similar characteristic may trigger feeding. Using that previous example of the Pale Morning Dun, a size 18 Royal Wulff's wings might trigger a trout's feeding imprint, even though it is feeding on something different now. Try attractor flies size 16 to 22, even over selective trout. You might be surprised.

Along the same lines, the way a trout perceives your fly might be completely different than how you might. This perception factor explains why a trout might take a Royal Wulff for a flying ant or a Humpy for a caddis. A Humpy can simulate many different foods like ants, beetles, caddis, mayflies, grasshoppers, etc. One thing to think about is that even though

A beautiful 28 inch rainbow caught by Bob Johnson at the top of Box Canyon on a small caddis fly. Photo by Bob Johnson.

Light rods of 2 to 5 weight with 8 to 9 foot lengths are preferred. Floating lines with 9 to 15 foot long leaders are all you need on the flat water. Use leaders with long, light, supple tippets (3 to 5 feet long) of 4X to 6X material to help overcome the effects of the intricate currents.

Fast Water Nymphing

Charlie Brooks, in his book on the Henry's Fork, popularized nymphing fast water with a high rod technique and sinking lines. It does still catch fish but is not done much anymore because a system with a floating line, strike indicator and a 9 to 12 foot leader is generally more effective, easier to master and more versatile. It allows natural drift, less weight on the fly and visual strike detection.

This method calls for 5 to 7 weight rods of an 8 1/2 to 9 1/2 foot length. Big nymphs in places like Box or Cardiac Canyons are often fished on 3X to 1X tippets to help handle the rocks and big trout encountered there. Place the strike indicator on the leader butt about 1 1/2 to 2 times the water depth from the fly or flies.

I like to use two flies much of the time because it gives the fish a choice and covers more water. Do this by tying on tippet material with a double surgeon's knot and leaving the lower tag end of the knot attached as a dropper. Occasionally you will catch a double.

I recall one day on Box Canyon when I was fishing a deep channel and hooked a good sized trout. I played it for a while and it felt really big but when it flipped on the surface it was just a 15 incher. I was confused just for a second...then the line shot away from me and a 5 pounder leaped into the air, dragging the 15 incher along with it. It was a fun double and the 1X tippet helped me land both fish in the fast water.

Use weighted nymphs and if you are never getting the bottom, add a removable B or BB split shot to the leader above the dropper for extra weight. Stand straight across from your target area and cast up-and-across stream, preferably with a reach mend and tuck cast. Allow enough drift area so the nymphs can sink into the strike zone (lower third, depthwise) before it reaches the target area. Remember that you are not actually fishing until the flies get down to the trout's feeding level. If you're not getting down, you're not catching many trout.

If the line bellies downstream, mend the line upstream and immediately feed some slack out from the rod tip so it can continue its drift without any unnatural drag. As the strike indicator bobs in the current, concentrate on its subtle drift clues. It should be the same speed or slightly slower than the surface

Falls River near Cave Falls and a forest fire in the corner of Yellowstone Park.

———————◆———————

currents (compare it to the bubbles on the water). If it's faster, you're dragging too much. Line manipulation is critical for a natural drift. Watch the indicator for a slight hesitation and set the hook on anything. Never assume it's just a rock or weed or you'll miss many trout.

Streamers in Rivers

Streamers often account for fewer fish but much bigger trout. They can be fished everywhere, including the flat waters of the ranch (floating lines) but are most effective on fast water sections like Box Canyon or Coffee Pot Rapids. The big flies used suggest rods of 6 to 8 weight and maybe a sink-tip line with short, stout leaders. I seldom fish streamers with anything lighter than 2X tippet and often 0X.

The basic technique is to cast across or down-and-across and strip the line in at a moderately fast retrieve while pointing the rod tip right at the fly. Keep the rod tip close to the water or actually under water so you can feel the light taps of chasing fish. Light taps usually mean fish are just nipping at the tail. Wait until you feel a distinct pull before you strike, otherwise you will pull it away from many fish. If you are fishing

from a boat, cast into shore and make 4 or 5 strips and recast if nothing chases. When wading, cast to the center of the river or to the bank and retrieve until the fly is hanging straight downstream or until it is close to the rod tip.

Sometimes a dead-drift swing is best. Just cast down-and-across and let the fly swing in the current, steelhead style. Many variations in retrieve are possible and none are wrong. Experiment until you find one that works especially well. Fishing streamers means that you will cover lots of water. Keep moving unless you keep getting hits in one area. The more water you cover, the more opportunistic fish you will find.

Two-Fly Techniques

I already mentioned fishing two nymphs at once but there are many other variations that are effective. On flat water, try one adult insect imitation and one emerger or nymph below it. Rig them by tying tippet material (5 inches to 3 feet long) to the dry fly hook bend or hook eye with a regular clinch knot. Then tie a nymph, emerger, ant, beetle, scud etc. to the tag end. Fish this rig as you would a dry fly but if the dry fly suddenly disappears, set the hook. The dry fly can catch trout but it also acts like a strike indicator for the other fly.

It is also the best way I know to fish really small dry flies and emergers that are impossible to see on the water. Just watch the bigger fly and if you see a rise about where the smaller fly is, set the hook. If you have avoided fishing small flies because you could not track the fly, try this technique. It's effective and easy. Thousands of combinations are possible, use your imagination. I especially like this technique for fishing a caddis adult with a trailing caddis pupa. It can be dead-drifted naturally or swung and skittered in faster currents.

———————◆———————

The spotted coralroot gets its nourishment from the decaying organic matter in the many lodgepole forests around the Henry's Fork.

A line-up of feathered fishers on Henry's Lake at the County Boat Ramp.

It can often outproduce a standard retrieve. Cutthroat trout are caught at all levels of the lake but the bigger hybrids prefer to feed just above weed beds.

Most of the time, 6 to 8 weight rods are used if it's windy. Floating lines are effective when fish are shallow but you need a type II sinking line to fish the typical 4 to 10 foot depths. Your third line should be a fast sinker (Hi-D) line. When fish go deep, you need to sometimes get down 10 to 15 feet deep. If fish are feeding over shallow water or over weed beds, a type I line or glass (slime) type line is also handy.

Remember that the heavier weight the fly line, the faster it sinks, even in the same type. For example: a type II, 8 weight sinks about the same as a type III, 6 weight. If you are using fast retrieves or fishing deep, you can use fast sinking lines. If you are fishing flies slowly or shallowly, pick a slower sinking line. Vary the retrieves from a slow crawl to a long, fast strip. Hesitate occasionally and speed up the retrieve once in a while to see if the variation produces hits from fish that are just following.

Pick dark colored flies during low light periods and smaller, light colored flies during bright, sunny conditions. Use 1X or 2X tippets early in the season and gradually reduce that size to 3X or 4X tippets later, as the fish get more selective. Fish one larger and one smaller fly until you find an effective pattern.

◆

Stillwater Strategies

Henry's Lake, Island Park Reservoir and Ashton Reservoir all provide chances for big trout. I suggest using a float tube, kick boat or fishing boat for any of these waters since wade fishing these stillwaters are usually spotty at best.

I like to fish small lake flies (size 14 to 8 hooks) when fishing is slow because the trout will be less selective on the small flies. I also enjoy using a long, stiff 4 weight or 5 weight rod if it's not too windy. Sinking lines are sometimes hard to find in these lighter weights but I'm convinced that they fish small stillwater flies with more finesse and sensitivity.

One technique that works well with bead-head nymphs is the vertical presentation. A floating line and long (10 to 15 foot) 4X tapered leader is needed. Small strike indicators at the end of the fly line also help. Just cast out into a good looking spot such as a channel between weed beds. Allow the nymph to sink for 15 to 60 seconds. Make several strips, which brings the fly straight up. If nothing hits, allow it to sink again and repeat. Watch the strike indicator closely as the fly sinks because the fly is often taken on the sink. Most lake fish have not seen this presentation and it can be very effective when traditional leech type fishing is slow.

A popular retrieve is to slowly kick your craft as you slowly retrieve the fly, just above the weed beds. The right sink-rate fly line is critical.

Another effective technique calls for a light wind and a craft that can drift with the wind. Cast into the wind or at angles to it and let the wind drift you, dragging the fly slowly.

◆

A meadow near Warm River Springs and an afternoon thunderhead.

Fly Patterns and Hatches

Choosing fly patterns can be as easy as asking the local fly shop what has been working on the stretch you want to fish, or by letting the guide select for you. If you are on your own, it can be much more complex. Observation is often the key. Look closely at the water and see if there are insect adults on the water. Check their size, shape and color against the imitation you have. If your bug is too big, that could be the answer to your problem. Also see if several insects are on the water at the same time. Each trout could be feeding on a different insect or stage of insect.

One way to eliminate the guesswork is to use a stomach pump on a trout you have caught. If used properly, it does not hurt the fish. You receive an education very quickly. Something else to try is an insect screen. The insect screen is just a window screen connected to two sticks. Place the screen in the water and disturb the weeds and rocks upstream of the screen.

Some stoneflies caught resting on neoprene waders in the morning. Prolific hatches have made the Henry's Fork legendary among fly fishers.

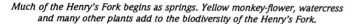

Much of the Henry's Fork begins as springs. Yellow monkey-flower, watercress and many other plants add to the biodiversity of the Henry's Fork.

Insects from a screen sample at Last Chance shows some of the aquatic food available to trout.

A Callibaetis *mayfly drifting a quiet side channel on the "Ranch."*

Raise the screen and see what nymphs and other aquatic edibles are available in the area. Lay your imitations next to the naturals and see how close you are.

Adult and emerging insects can be screened as well. Just leave the screen in the river for several minutes to catch naturally drifting trout foods. It's a good way to catch and observe emergers. It is fascinating to watch the metamorphosis as they hatch.

Use the hatch chart provided to guess at what should be hatching but remember that hatches can be early, late or almost non-existant depending on weather conditions, water temperature, river flows etc. Remember that there are several stages of each insect as well. Nymph, emerger, dun and spinner stages can be imitated in many instances. Here again, local fly shop knowledge is invaluable. They can tell you where and what time of day to fish which stage of insect. This is by no means a complete list, which would require a whole book by itself.

Basic Hatch Information for the Henry's Fork (alphabetical)

Brown Drake (*Ephemerella simulans*)	#10-12	June 25-July 5	Hatch in slow, silty sections of river, particularly lower Harriman State Park.
Caddis	#10-20	June and July	Entire river has good caddis hatches in faster water sections.
Golden Stone	#6-8	June	Found in all fast, rocky sections.
Gray Drake (*Siphlonurus occidentalis*)	#8-10	July and August	Ashton to Chester has phenomenal hatches. Harriman State Park in August.
Iron Blue Quill (*Baetis tricaudatus*)	#18	Spring and fall	If you come early or late you may see this mayfly.
Light Cahill (*Cinygma dimicki*)	#12	Mid-July	Seen from Mack's Inn to Osborne Bridge.
Mahogany Dun (*Paraleptophlebia bicornuta*)	#16-18		One of September's best hatches.
Pale Morning Dun (*Ephemerella infrequens*)	#16-18	June 10-June 30	From Last Chance to St. Anthony.
Pale Morning Dun (*Ephemerella inermis*)	#18-20	July 15-September 1	Duns appear mid-morning, spinner falls evening and morning.
Salmonfly (*Pteronarcys californica*)	#4	May-June	This popular hatch starts in the lower, warmer reaches and progresses upstream, reaching Box Canyon about the first week of June. Available in fast, rocky sections.
Small Western Drake (*Ephemerella flavilinea*)	#14-16	July 1-July 25	Loves cloudy days.
Snowflake Dun (*Ephoron album*)	#12-14		Occurs below Ashton Dam in late October.
Speckled Spinner (*Callibaetis nigritus*)	#14-16	July and August	Look for them on quiet sections of Henry's Fork and area lakes.
Tiny Blue Quill (*Baetis parvus*)	#20-22	Late June and July	Good hatches in upper Harriman State Park.
Tiny Blue-Winged Olive (*Pseudocloeon edmundsi*)		#22-24	July 15-October 15. Some blanket hatches occur in September, especially on cloudy, rainy days.
Western Green Drake (*Ephemerella grandis*)	#8-10	June 23-July 1	Most popular hatch and very fun to fish but hard to predict. Best action is on upper ranch and Last Chance area.
White Wing Black (*Tricorythodes minutus*)	#20-22		Good August hatch. Morning spinner fall.

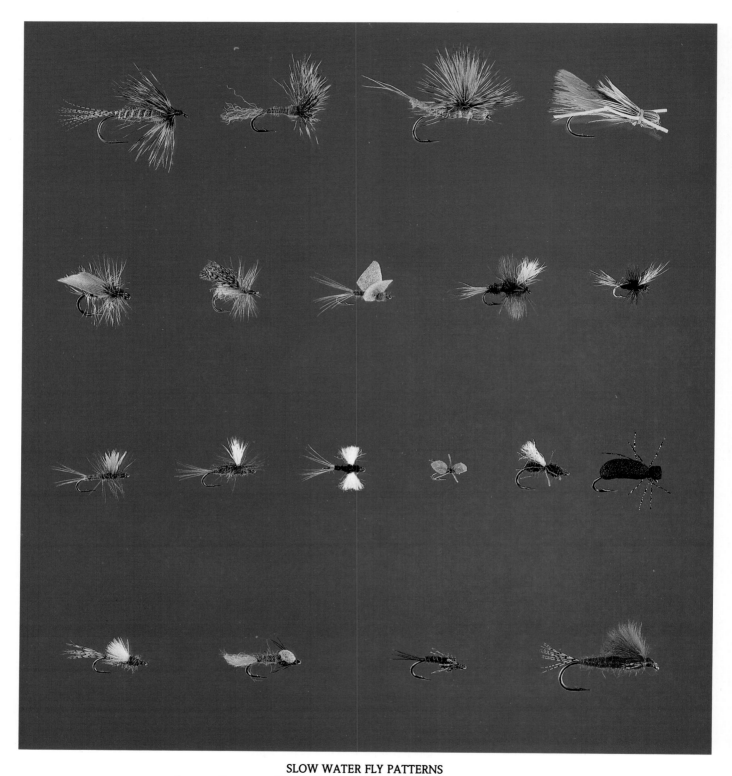

SLOW WATER FLY PATTERNS
Lawson Emerger   Sparkle Dun   Green Paradrake   Henry's Fork Hopper
Henryville Caddis   Partridge Caddis   No-Hackle   Royal Wulff   Humpy
Thorax Dun   Olive Parachute   Spent Spinner   Foam Ant   Flying Ant   Foam Beetle
Harrop Emerger   Floating Nymph   Pheasant Tail Nymph   Brown Drake Nymph

FAST WATER FLY PATTERNS

California Trude   Royal Wulff   Stimulator   Bullet-Head Stone   Adams   Elk Hair Caddis

Rabbit Strip Streamer   Wiggle Bug   Willard Fly   Rubber-Leg Stone

Gold Ribbed Hare's Ear   Chamois Caddis   LaFontaine Caddis Pupa   Prince Nymph   San Juan Worm   Peeking Caddis   Egg Pattern

STILL WATER FLY PATTERNS

Marabou Leech   Woolly Bugger   Crystal Bugger   Spruce Streamer

Peacock Woolly Worm   Mohair Leech   Canadian Brown   Mickey Finn   Tullis Wiggle Damsel

Goddard Caddis   Scud   Damsel Nymph   Peacock Snail   Hare's Ear   Prince Nymph   Peacock Nymph

Attractions and Tributaries

No trip to the Henry's Fork would be complete without a side trip to one of the wonderful areas nearby. There are many trails for hiking, wilderness lakes and streams to backpack to, beautiful environs to vegitate near, wildlife to observe and organized entertainment to attend.

Yellowstone National Park is less than an hour away. The Park alone has more waters than an angler could fish in a year. The Yellowstone, Slough, Bechler, Madison, Firehole, Gallitan, Falls, Lamar, Gardner, Gibbon, Lewis and many other streams provide thousands of miles of rivers and creeks to fish. Many lakes also have excellent angling opportunities. Its thermal features are world famous and was once called Coulter's Hell, after a mountain man who travelled through and described the place to an unbelieving audience.

Just south of Yellowstone are the Tetons and the Wind River Range. North is the Beartooths and one of the most incredible highways you could ever drive. Each have an impressive array of mountains, hiking trails, trout streams, mountain lakes and tourist attractions. In fact, there is so much country to explore within several hours drive of the Henry's Fork that

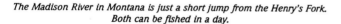

The Madison River in Montana is just a short jump from the Henry's Fork. Both can be fished in a day.

The weather can change hourly in this mountainous region so be prepared for anything from hot, sunny weather to a summer snowstorm. Highway 20 is your best bet for Henry's Fork access.

I'd be willing to bet that no one person could fish it all in a lifetime of trying. This area has been called the golden circle because of all the prime fly fishing opportunities available in a 100 mile circle.

The Henry's Fork itself has several tributaries that provide excellent fishing in addition to the main river. In other parts of the country, some of these waters would be considered top notch fisheries, but here the locals regard them little and touring anglers usually stick to the famous sections of river.

The Buffalo River, which flows by Pond's Lodge and into Box Canyon, is full of small trout and is planted with larger hatchery fish. It is a great place to take kids to teach them to fly fish. There are nearly always fish rising there.

The Warm River is a pretty spring creek that sees little fishing pressure and is a good place to get away from it all. The river bursts out of the ground at the old Warm River hatchery and flows through a wilderness canyon for 6 or 7 miles until flowing into the Henry's Fork just below Bear Gulch Canyon. It has mostly smaller trout that take attractor dry flies readily. The best water is below the springs and down in the canyon in an area called the "tunnel" after an old railroad tunnel that can be seen from the Mesa Falls Scenic Drive. Expect to do some hiking.

The Falls River is a major tributary that strengthens the Henry's Fork at Chester Backwaters. It is famous mostly because of its beautiful falls upstream but also because its headwaters are called the Bechler River, which some of you may have heard of. This wilderness stream flows out of the southwest corner of Yellowstone Park and has been known to produce rainbow trout of 6 to 10 pounds. It also has many cutthroat trout. If you like fishing high elevation lakes, this is another good area. A recent fire may impact this watershed. The lower section of the Falls River is nearly dried up because of irrigation demands but the upper parts are still pristine.

The Teton River gained national infamy when the Teton Dam busted, flooding several towns, killing 9 people and causing a billion dollars damage. The river is coming back nicely now and the upper portion is unhurt. Access is sometimes difficult so float fishing is best, a good area map will show how to get there and farmers will usually let you cross their land if you ask. Much of it is a meadow-like stream but there are some unfloatable canyon stretches.

How to Save a River

The Henry's Fork has had its share of problems in the past and continues to now. Perhaps there is no easy answer but there is a core of concerned people that have made it a goal to make sure this river remains one of the best fisheries in the world. The following is a brief overview of current problems that are being analyzed and dealt with.

When the first settlers arrived in the Island Park area, they found the river and springs teeming with native cutthroat trout. They were harvested for food and fertilizer. Harry Stampp, an early settler where the Flat Rock Club is now located, used a boat at night rigged with lanterns that would attract trout to their glow. He would then spear them and fill his boat. There was an abundance of 1/2 to 6 pound cutthroat then, with occasional larger fish. Several private hatcheries were run on the river and its springs, producing trout for sale.

Rainbows that the river is famous for were introduced by them and by subsequent stockings. They were a strong breed of fish that came from the Hayspur hatchery and reached larger sizes than the cutthroat trout. They interbred with the remnants of the native cutthroat populations and this rainbow/cutthroat hybrid became the predominant trout of the area. Most resident Henry's Fork rainbows today have faint cutthroat trout markings still.

The trout population has fluctuated considerably in the last 30 years. Most long-time Henry's Fork anglers agree that the mid 70s to 1982 were the best years in recent history. It was considered by many to be the best dry fly fishing in the world;

Anglers from Three Rivers Ranch test the waters below Cave Falls.

1993 was also a very good year for big fish but that was due to the 1992 drawdown of Island Park Reservoir which flushed many trout out of the lake and into the river, mixing many hatchery fish with the wild trout population. The drawdown at the end of the season was so Fish and Game could treat the reservoir most economically.

The hatchery holdovers are beginning to feed more like the other resident trout now but most anglers can tell the difference in the trouts' fighting abilities and appearance. Most fly rodders see the generally poor genetic quality of todays hatchery trout to be considerably inferior to wild trout populations and do not wish to see supplemental stocking of the river. "Wild Trout!" is their battle call.

Another big cause for concern was the release of 50,000 tons of silt into the river system when the reservoir drawdown occurred. As the lake lowered, the river at the upper end of the reservoir cut a channel throught the silt that had been accumulating. The silt had nowhere to go but into the river. It filled many holes in the slower water. Harriman State Park or "the Ranch" was the most noticable. Many of the deeper holes were completely filled and there became less diversity of terrain, less structure for the trout.

The river was flushed to help remove the silt and the result was it scoured part of the river. Much of the aquatic vegetation

---◆---

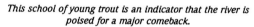

This school of young trout is an indicator that the river is poised for a major comeback.

was gone and even some of the islands in the river were lost. The weed beds have a tendency to fill the center of the river, concentrating the current along the banks and creating good currents through wide sections and in back channels. The elimination of the weeds caused a more uniform flow in the center of the river that left many fringe areas that previously had good current, stagnant. Many anglers wondered if they had seen the last of the river's once legendary fishing and hatches.

Despite the drastic change to the river, the scouring caused by the silt being flushed out of the river seems to have had less effect on the long term health of the river as one might think. The hatches have changed some but the weed beds are coming back nicely and many of the areas that were clogged with silt are now flushed clean again.

Another threat to the weed beds was created by an overpopulation of trumpeter swans and other waterfowl that wintered in Harriman State Park and fed on the weeds. From 1988 through 1990 the river had little aquatic vegetation. The aquatic vegetation (macrophytes) shrunk to almost nothing. Young trout need cover from predators and they had little. Low water and cold conditions caused icing of the river. In a misguided effort to save the swans, the river was flushed to break the ice free. The resulting ice flows gouged up even more vegetation and flushed many trout downstream, causing displacement if not death. Many swans died anyway so now they are trapped and moved to prevent overpopulation.

This episode helps illustrate the lack of unity between water and wildlife management. The river has not been managed as one entity. Each group has its own agenda and that is all they try to do, the river is not managed as one living, breathing ecosystem.

The section of river that holds the most promise, but also has the biggest problems, is the lower section. It is totally managed for water rights only, as irrigation water for farms. High waters upstream become dry streambeds from St. Anthony downstream. Very little water is left in the original river channel. It is diverted through a large series of canals. Since trout must go where the water goes, most of the trout get trapped in the canals during summer. In fall, the canals are turned off, drying up the places trout were. It has been legal to collect truckloads of trout that are dead or dying in the dried up canals.

If the lower river were managed with fish screens on the canals, a minimum instream flow and some sportsman's accesses provided, it could rival the best trout fisheries anywhere. The water has beautiful runs, riffles, pools, pocket water and backwaters. Some springs feed the river here but are on private property. The trout are here, and some big ones, but access is tough in this whole stretch and few anglers know their way around the private property, diversion dams and braided waterways.

Several other factors enter into the picture. The river below Island Park Reservoir is sometimes completely shut off. The only thing that saves the Henry's Fork is the Buffalo River (which comes in just below the dam) and a few small springs. Water flows are clearly one of the major problems of the river.

Another is the unstable watershed caused by logging prac-

Fish population surveys indicate that the Henry's Fork is set to provide good fishing for a long time. Problems the river has are being dealt with and the fishing is responding positively, but the vigil has just begun.

tices. When the trees are cleared, watersheds become stressed. The snows melt much quicker, causing increased erosion. The silt is then deposited into streams, stiffling hatches and ruining spawning substrate. The siltation also contributes to increased water temperatures. Water temperatures that fluctuate too much will not only mess up the timing of hatches but kill many insects. Once the biomass in the river is reduced, trout respond by becoming fewer and smaller. Warm water also stresses the trout by depleting their ability to extract oxygen.

If these things are not enough, the river has also been under the threat of hydroelectric power development. A new facility has been installed at Island Park Dam and is now functioning. The jury is still out on if it will change the fishery in any way. Cardiac Canyon (Riverside to Warm River) is one of the most beautiful and wild canyons in the region. The Corps of Engineers could go wild on this section of river, and the government has proposed several projects. Luckily the projects have been stopped for now but they need to be watched.

Ranching has been going on, even in the sensitive lands of Harriman State Park for some time. The Harrimans I'm sure were quite good at rotating grazing areas to keep cattle from overgrazing any one area, but the governmental agencies that run the park now seem oblivious to the concept. Overgrazing streambanks caused erosion. The once undercut, grassy banks

became muddy banks with little cover, allowing water temperatures to increase and eliminating many of the areas where young trout can hide and grow. The Henry's Fork Foundation has funded a fencing project that is now keeping cattle away from fragile banks but the degradation that has already occurred will take a while to repair itself.

Not long ago it became necessary to improve the sewer system for the settlements along the river. Improper sewage treatment had caused water quality to deteriorate in the water table. Many cabins still have inadequate septic systems but much of the problem has been halted.

Those who visited Big Springs in 1994 were probably disappointed because trout that once fed on bread or trout pellets thrown them are gone now. I heard word that snowmobilers had gone in during winter and poisoned the trout. The fish and game department of many states, not just Idaho, seem to put a much higher priority on research than on enforcement. Much of the Henry's Fork has special regulations but fish wardens are almost nonexistent. I have never been checked for my licence in all the years I've fished and guided the river, although I've heard of a few that have. Most anglers can tell stories of encounters with law breakers that don't care about regulations. Officers do go to Henry's Lake en masse once or twice a year and write dozens of tickets a day. One fellow was caught with

47

57 fish in his boat. While it is true that special regulation waters tend to be self regulating because of the sportsman-like conduct of the average angler, law breakers do impact the fishery negatively.

Are we depressed yet? Well, don't be. I've related these things to you because change cannot occur if we don't know the problems. Many changes have already started to occur in the minds of those who can make a difference and mother nature has remarkable powers of regeneration as well. Nearly everyone I talked to about the river was discouraged about the past but optimistic that things are poised for a remarkable rebound.

The Henry's Fork Foundation is engaged in many projects such as: fishery shelters, winter concealment cover for juvenile trout, riparian fencing for bank and streamside protection, stream flow monitoring and alarm, studies on the effect of win-

ter on trout and also had a successful lobby for catch-and-release fishing on certain river stretches. Please join them even if you never visit the river. Each membership is an increase in the voice heard by lawmakers. Contact Henry's Fork Foundation at: P.O. Box 61, Island Park, Idaho 83429. Ph. 208-558-9041.

The Henry's Fork is a remarkable river and truly one of this nation's treasures. I believe that the conditions of the waters we rely on are an indication of the overall health of our ecosystem and our world. There are physical, mental, economical and spiritual considerations for which rivers play a part in each of our lives. Negative things do occur but if good people do nothing but stand idly by, just lamenting, they are part of the problem, not the solution. Which is why I'd like to see you visit the Henry's Fork. It's difficult to calculate a treasure you have not experienced.

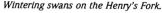

Wintering swans on the Henry's Fork.